SO DELICIOUS

LESS CALORIES, MORE FLAVOR

Johanna Hurmerinta

SO DELICIOUS LESS CALORIES, MORE FLAVOR © 2024 Johanna Hurmerinta. All rights reserved. No part of this book may be used or reproduced in any manner without written permission. The only exception is in the case of brief quotations embodied in book reviews. For more information, please contact by email johanna@hurmerinta.com

Photography by Johanna Hurmerinta

Recipes by Johanna Hurmerinta

Designed by Johanna Hurmerinta

Editing: An editor team in the US

Publisher: Johanna Hurmerinta

Distributor: IngramSpark

ISBN hardcopy: 978-952-65047-2-8

CONTENTS

INTRODUCTION 4

SALADS 8

SIDE DISH / STARTER 20

SHRIMP AND PRAWNS. 28

SALMON 38

WHITE LEAN FISH 58

CHICKEN 66

MEAT 80

DESSERT 90

HEALTHY FOOD 98

IF YOU HAVE DIABETES 99

INTRODUCTION

My new cookbook follows the same theme as my first cookbook MIGHTY DELICIOUS.

The recipes are for healthy meals with fresh ingredients, which are rich in flavor. This cookbook is for everyone, who loves delicious and healthy food, and especially for people who are interested in diabetes-friendly and heart-healthy food.

The recipes in this book offer a wide variety of meals based on Scandinavian cooking. I have also included some recipes for Mediterranean and Asian meals. With chapters like fresh salads, vegetable dishes, fish, chicken, whole-grain pasta, lean meat and dessert, I hope you find many new favorites to enjoy. To eat less salt, unhealthy fat and sugar, helps to maintain a healthy weight and improve your health.

Most recipes are for low-carb and low-sugar meals without sacrificing taste. This cookbook offers many fish recipes, especially salmon recipes. Salmon is rich in long-chain omega-3 fatty acids, which have been shown to reduce inflammation and lower blood pressure. Salmon contains protein and vitamin D. To eat salmon at least once a week is a healthy decision. In addition it is good to eat white lean fish once a week or more often.

I have included asparagus, avocado, tomato and broccoli in quite many recipes. The reason is their health benefits.

Asparagus spears are packed with nutrients, providing a good source of fiber, vitamin C and folate. Asparagus is also an excellent source of vitamin K.

One of broccoli's biggest advantages is its nutrient content. It's loaded with a wide array of vitamins, minerals and fiber.

Tomatoes are low in calories and high in nutrients including potassium and vitamins A and C.

Avocados are high in healthy fats and contain vitamin K, vitamin C, potassium, vitamins B5 and B6, and also vitamin E.

Herbs like watercress, basil, lemon balm and peas shoots are filled with vitamins. Add herbs to your meal as often as you can.

Nowadays there are so much we have to fit into our busy lives. Sometimes we don't have time to cook for one hour or more. My recipes are due to this mostly very easy to do and you can cook them in just 20-30 minutes.

I wish to inspire you to test new ingredients and spices. All the ingredients in my recipes are available in Europe, the US and in many other countries. Be creative, be brave and have fun when you cook.

This book is for everyone who wants to enjoy healthy and delicious food every day or a few times per week. I hope you love the recipes, and I hope this book inspires you to eat more fruit, vegetables, fish and lean meat.

Johanna Hurmerinta
Espoo, Finland
August 2024

ALL RECIPES SERVE TWO

I have made the recipes for two people. If you cook just for yourself, you can either do the recipe as it is and have a delicious meal also for the next day, or you can choose to use half of the amount of the ingredients in the recipe.

If you cook for four people, you can double everything except the spices. With spices it's best to taste how much is needed. Always taste while you cook. It is the only way to learn how much you want of each spice.

SUBSTITUTES AND THE SIZE OF A DISH

I have added substitutes in many recipes. They are examples of what you might want to change to, due to a special diet or when seasonal ingredients can be harder to find. Remember, you can always subsitute anything in the recipe to something you prefer or have at home.

My recipes are for meals, which are large enough if you eat the healthy way (every four hours). If you want to, you can always make a larger dish. It all depends on how hungry you are.

COOKING MEASUREMENTS AND ABBREVIATIONS

This book is published in many countries. I have added the US, the UK and the European measurements in the recipes.

Teaspoon = **tsp**   Tablespoon = **tbsp**   Ounce = **Oz**   Milliliter = **ml**   Grams = **g**

GREAT INGREDIENTS TO HAVE FOR COOKING

I suggest you have these wonderful basic ingredients at home. I use many of these in my recipes.

Olive oil. Extra virgin olive oil.

Apple cider vinegar and balsamic vinegar. (If you can find honey vinegar, try it). Balsamic glaze.

Salt. Soy sauce.

Green and black olives in brine.

Cans (jars): Chopped tomatoes, asparagus, corn and mushrooms.

Spices:

Dried thyme, dried dill, dried basil and dried oregano.

Ground black pepper. Crushed red pepper (also called ground pink pepper).

Lemon pepper seasoning. Chili powder.

Roasted Garlic & Pepper seasoning.

Tomato & Pepper Seasoning. (Many brands include also basil in this seasoning.)

Garlic paste. Ginger paste. Chili paste.

SALADS

MOZZARELLA ASPARAGUS AND TOMATO

2 mozzarella balls

10 fresh asparagus spears (or spears in can)

8-12 cherry tomatoes

1 cup (240 g) chopped mixed lettuce

8-12 basil leaves (or lemon balm leaves)

2 tbsp extra virgin olive oil

1 tsp ground black pepper

1 tsp dried thyme

How to prepare:

Discard the hard stem of the asparagus. Usually 1-2 inches. Cook the asparagus (unless you use spears from a can) in boiling water for 5-6 minutes. Add a sprinkle of salt to the water. Divide the chopped lettuce between two plates.

Cut the mozzarella balls in half. Place 2 halves on each plate. Cut the asparagus spears in half lengthwise and add the asparagus on the cheese. Cut the tomatoes into slices and these on the plates. Add basil leaves on both salads. Use small or large leaves.

Season with olive oil, dried thyme and black pepper. Tomato & Pepper seasoning is also a great choice.

DID YOU KNOW: ORIGINAL MOZZARELLA CHEESE IS MADE FROM WATER BUFFALO MILK. IT DOES NOT CONTAIN LACTOSE (LIKE THE MILK FROM A COW). IT IS THUS A GREAT CHOICE FOR LACTOSE INTOLERANT PEOPLE.

AVOCADO PEACH TOMATO AND SCALLION

1 avocado

1 cup (240 g) sliced lettuce (cosmopolitan, romaine, or iceberg)

12 small tomatoes

1 can (tin) peach slices

1 scallion / spring onion

1 tsp dried basil or thyme

1 tsp crushed red pepper

1 tsp lemon pepper seasoning

How to prepare:

Divide the sliced lettuce between two plates.

Cut the avocado in half. Remove the stone and cut the fruit into small chunks. Wash the tomatoes and cut them in half. Divide the avocados and the tomatoes between the plates.

Cut the peach slices in half. Add peach chunks on both plates. Wash the spring onion and cut it into thin slices. Divide these between the plates. Cut the lemon in half. Sprinkle lemon juice on the salads.

Season with dried herbs, red pepper and lemon pepper. (If red pepper is too spicy for you, a good substitute is tomato and basil seasoning.)

AVOCADO RADISH TOMATO AND BASIL

1 cup (240 g) chopped lettuce

1 avocado

10-12 cherry tomatoes

2 radishes

1 scallion / spring onion

14-20 basil leaves

2 tbsp extra virgin olive oil

1 lemon

1 tsp Tomato & Pepper seasoning

1 tsp dried thyme

How to prepare:

Divide the lettuce slices between two plates. Cut the avocado in half. Remove the stone and cut the fruit into small chunks. Divide the avocado between the plates.

Cut the radishes into thin slices. Cut some of the tomatoes in half. Divide radish, tomato and basil between the plates. Peel the scallion, chop off the root part and slice the rest. Add scallion on the salad.

Cut the lemon in half. Season the salads with olive oil, lemon juice, dried thyme and pepper.

DID YOU KNOW: AVOCADOS ARE A SOURCE OF VITAMINS C, E, K, AND B6, AS WELL AS RIBOFLAVIN, NIACIN, FOLATE, PANTOTHENIC ACID, MAGNESIUM, AND POTASSIUM. THEY ALSO PROVIDE LUTEIN, BETA CAROTENE, AND OMEGA-3 FATTY ACIDS. AVOCADOS CONTAIN HIGH LEVELS OF HEALTHY, BENEFICIAL FATS, WHICH CAN HELP A PERSON FEEL FULLER BETWEEN MEALS.

CARROT TOMATO BLUEBERRIES AND BASIL

20 arugula leaves

10-14 basil leaves

2 radishes

1 scallion

10 cherry tomatoes

8 olives

1 large carrot

4 tbsp blueberries

2 tbsp extra virgin olive oil

1 tbsp vinegar (apple or honey)

1 tsp Tomato & Pepper seasoning

1 tsp dried oregano

How to prepare:

Divide the arugula leaves between two plates. Add basil leaves on top.

Cut the radishes into thin slices and add them on the basil. Peel and cut the scallion into thin slices (remove first the hard root part) and add the slices on the salads. Add the tomatoes and the olives. Peel the carrot. Slice it thinly and add the slices in the middle of the salad.

Season with olive oil, vinegar, pepper seasoning and dried oregano.

Garnish with delicious blueberries for extra vitamins and antioxidants.

AVOCADO BASIL PESTO AND BERRIES

10-14 strawberries

1 avocado

8-12 cherry tomatoes

2 radishes

20 basil leaves (or pea shoots)

4 tsp pesto

How to prepare:

Cut the avocado in half. Remove the stone and cut the fruit into small chunks. Wash the tomatoes and cut them in half. Divide the avocado and the tomatoes between two plates.

Cut the strawberries into halves. Remove the green part. Cut the radishes into thin slices. Divide the berries and the radish slices between the plates.

Add basil leaves on both plates. Season with pesto.

DID YOU KNOW: PEA SHOOTS HAVE A MILD, SWEET FLAVOUR WITH A GRASSY, NUTTY UNDERTONE. PEA SHOOTS ARE RICH IN VITAMINS AND MINERALS INCLUDING VITAMIN C, IRON AND CALCIUM.

AVOCADO EGGS TOMATO AND THYME

1 avocado
2 eggs
8-10 cherry or other small tomatoes
6 lettuce leaves

4-6 fresh thyme sprigs
4 tsp pesto
1 tsp dried basil
1 tsp lemon pepper seasoning

How to prepare:

Cook the eggs in boiling water for 6 minutes. Wash the lettuce leaves and cut them into slices. Divide the lettuce slices between two plates.

Cut the avocado in half. Remove the stone and cut the fruit into small chunks. Divide the avocados and the tomatoes between the plates. Add pesto on some of the avocado chunks. Season with fresh thyme.

Drain the eggs and keep them in cold water for 1 minute. Then it is easier to peel them. Peel the eggs and cut them into quarters. Add these on the salads.

Season with dried basil and lemon pepper.

SIDE DISH / STARTER

PROSCIUTTO AVOCADO AND MELON

7 oz (200 g) prosciutto
(or any cured ham you like)

1 avocado

1 honeydew or cantaloupe melon

2 tsp pesto

2 tbsp sun-dried tomato slices

1 scallion or green onion

1 tsp lemon pepper seasoning

Thick balsamic glaze OR

the juice of one lemon

How to prepare:

Cut the prosciutto into small slices. Divide the slices between two plates. Cut the avocado in half, remove the stone, and cut the fruit into small chunks. Divide these between the plates.

Wash the green onion (or scallion). Chop off the root part and the top of the green part and cut the main part into thin slices. Add the slices on the avocado. Cut the melon in half. Scrape off the seeds. Cut the halves into 1 inch (25 mm) slices. Cut off the skin tracing the curve of the melon with your knife. Cut the fruit into small chunks and add these on the plates.

Add the sun-dried tomato slices on the salads. Season with lemon pepper seasoning and balsamic glaze (or lemon juice, which is also a great choice).

TOMATO ASPARAGUS AND SOUR CREAM

1 large (beefsteak) tomato

8 asparagus spears

¼ tsp salt

6 olives (black or green)

1 spring onion

2 large tbsp sour cream (or yogurt)

2 tbsp extra virgin olive oil

1 tsp dried basil or dried thyme

How to prepare:

This dish is best with a beefsteak tomato or another large size tomato. Cut off the hard part of the asparagus and cook the spears in boiling water for 5 minutes.

Wash and cut the tomato into thick slices. Use the largest slices for this dish. (You can eat the rest of the tomato later or chop it into small pieces and add to this dish.)

Cut the olives into slices. Cut off the bottom part of the spring onion and also the top green part. Cut the rest of the spring onion into slices.

Add 1 large tomato slice on each plate. Drain the asparagus and season the spears with a tiny bit of salt. Divide the spears between the two plates. Add the olives and the spring onion on the asparagus. Add 1 large tbsp of sour cream (or natural yogurt if you prefer) on each dish. Season with olive oil and dried herbs.

BROCCOLI ASPARAGUS MUSHROOM TOMATO

1 cup (240 g) broccoli florets

8 asparagus spears

½ tsp salt

10 mushrooms

1-2 tbsp chopped red onion

1 small can (tin) cherry tomatoes

1/2 cup (120 ml) water

1 tsp garlic paste

(Substitute: garlic powder)

1-2 tbsp grated parmesan

2 tsp dried basil

1 tsp Roasted Garlic & Pepper seasoning

How to prepare:

Pre-heat the oven to 390 F (200 C). Choose an oven pan with high sides. Add the tomatoes from the can in the pan. Add water and broccoli florets. Cut off the hard bottom part of the asparagus spears. Cut the spears into smaller pieces and add these in the pan.

Cut the mushrooms in half and add also these in the pan. Season with garlic paste (or garlic powder), dried basil and also Garlic & Pepper seasoning. Sprinkle chopped red onion on the dish.

Cook this vegetable dish in the oven for 18-20 minutes. Garnish with grated parmesan and divide between two plates.

(If you would like to add something more than vegetables to this dish, add a can of tuna.)

SALMON PEAS PRAWNS AND CUCUMBER

9 oz (250 g) cured or smoked salmon

6 prawns

1 tsp Tomato & Pepper seasoning

1 cucumber

½ cup (120 g) frozen, cooked peas

2 tbsp creme fraiche (sour cream)

2 tbsp chopped chives

Optional: A few drops of sweet chili sauce

How to prepare:

Pan-fry the prawns in oil on medium heat for 4 minutes. Turn the prawns after the first 2 minutes. Season with Tomato & pepper seasoning.

Warm up the frozen peas in boiling water for 2 minutes.

Discard the ends of the cucumber. Slice the cucumber and put the slices in a bowl with cold water.

Divide the salmon between two plates. Add the prawns on the salmon. Divide the cucumber and the peas between the plates.

Sprinkle chopped chives on the prawns and add a few drops of sweet chili sauce.

Add sour cream on the prawns.

SHRIMP/PRAWNS

AVOCADO PRAWNS TOMATO AND PESTO

1 avocado

1 cup (240 g) cooked, peeled prawns

14-16 cherry tomatoes

1 lemon

8-10 green olives

1 tsp lemon pepper seasoning

1 tsp dried thyme or basil

2 tsp pesto

Optional: 10 basil leaves or lemon balm leaves

How to prepare:

If you use frozen prawns, put them in the refrigerator a day before making this dish. This way the prawns are cold but not frozen. Cut the prawns in half.

Remove the stone from the avocado, use a spoon to get the fruit off the skin and cut the fruit into small pieces. Divide the avocado and the prawns between two plates. Cut the lemon in half and squeeze the juice on the avocado and prawns. Add the tomatoes, basil and the olives on the plates. Season with lemon pepper and dried herbs. Sprinkle pesto on the avocado chunks.

DID YOU KNOW: AVOCADOS ARE A SOURCE OF VITAMINS C, E, K, AND B6, AS WELL AS RIBOFLAVIN, NIACIN, FOLATE, MAGNESIUM, AND POTASSIUM. THEY ALSO PROVIDE LUTEIN, BETA CAROTENE, AND OMEGA-3 FATTY ACIDS. AVOCADOS CONTAIN HIGH LEVELS OF HEALTHY, BENEFICIAL FATS.

FRIED RICE PRAWNS AND BROCCOLI

1/2 cup (100 g) basmati or whole grain rice

2 tsp soy sauce

2 tsp sesame oil

1 tsp ground black pepper

1 egg

3 tbsp olive oil

8 broccoli florets

10-14 basil leaves

2 tbsp cashew nuts

10 cherry tomatoes

10-14 cooked prawns

How to prepare:

If you use frozen prawns, put them in the refrigerator one day before making this dish. Cook the rice according to the instructions on the package.

Cook the broccoli florets in boiling water until they are soft. (Frozen florets take less time to cook.) If the florets are large, cut them in half.

Whisk 1 egg in a small bowl. Cut the tomatoes in half. Drain the broccoli and the rice. Heat up a wok pan (or a pan with higher sides) to medium heat. Add the olive oil and the prawns. Cook for 1 minute. Turn the prawns. Add the rice, the broccoli, and the nuts. Cook for 2 minutes. Stir regularly. Add the whisked egg on one side of the pan and stir the egg so it cooks. Then mix it into the rice. Add sesame oil, soy sauce and pepper. Cook for 1 minute. Stir regularly.

Divide the fried rice between two plates. Garnish with basil leaves and tomatoes.

TOMATO SHRIMP PEA SPAGHETTI

5 oz (140 g) spaghetti (whole grain)
2 tbsp cream cheese (garlic flavor or herbs)
½ cup (120 g) frozen peas
6 cherry tomatoes
1 tsp lemon pepper

1 cup (240 g) cooked, peeled shrimp
1 tsp Ginger Chili & Lime seasoning
(or Ginger & Chili seasoning)
½ lemon
2 tsp dried basil

How to prepare:

Cook the spaghetti. Follow the instructions on the pasta package.

Cut the tomatoes in half. Cook the frozen peas and shrimp in boiling water for 1 minute.

When the spaghetti is ready, drain it and mix it with the cream cheese.

Divide the spaghetti between two plates or bowls. Add the shrimp, the peas and the tomatoes. Season with lemon juice and Ginger Chili & Lime seasoning or a similar spice. (Lemon pepper seasoning is a good substitute.)

Sprinkle dried basil on the dish for extra lovely flavor.

SHRIMP LEEK SALMON AND WATERCRESS

1 cup (240 g) peeled, cooked shrimp

5 oz (140 g) skinless salmon fillet

4 tbsp olive oil

½ tsp salt, 1 tsp lemon pepper seasoning

½ cup (120 ml) low-fat sour cream mixed with 2 tbsp lemon juice

6 cherry tomatoes

2 tbsp leek slices

2 radishes

1 tsp Tomato & Pepper seasoning (or similar)

3 oz (80 g) ready to eat watercress

1 tsp dried thyme

1 tsp dried dill

2 tbsp blueberries.

Optional: Raspberries

How to prepare:

If you use frozen shrimp, put them in the refrigerator one day before making this dish.

Slice the radish and the leek. Cut the tomatoes in half. Divide these between two plates. Season with 1 tbsp olive oil and Tomato & Pepper seasoning. Divide the crème fraiche (sour cream) between the two plates, next to the vegetables.

Cut the salmon fillet in half lengthwise and cut the slices into 1 inch (25 mm) pieces. Take a non-stick pan and cook the salmon in 3 tbsp olive oil on medium heat for 4 minutes. Flip the salmon after the first 2 minutes. Season with salt and lemon pepper seasoning.

Add the salmon on the crème fraiche (sour cream). Add the shrimp and the watercress. Season with the dried herbs. Garnish with berries.

PRAWNS EGGS AVOCADO AND SALMON

2 eggs

12 cooked, peeled prawns (cold, not frozen)

5 oz (140 g) skinless salmon fillet

3 tbsp olive oil

½ tsp salt

1 tsp lemon pepper seasoning

1 avocado

1 lemon

10 cherry tomatoes

8-12 basil leaves

2 tbsp fresh dill

1 tsp Tomato & Pepper seasoning

Optional: 6-8 strawberries

How to prepare:

Cook the eggs for 6-7 minutes. Transfer the eggs into cold water, so it is easier to peel them after a few minutes. Cut the eggs in half. Cut the salmon fillet into 1 inch (25mm) pieces. Heat up a non-stick pan to medium heat and cook the salmon in oil for 3 minutes. Turn the salmon and cook for 2 minutes. Season with salt and lemon pepper seasoning. Cut the avocado in half, remove the stone. Take the fruit off the skin. Mash the avocado.

Wash the strawberries and cut off the green stem. Cut the strawberries into halves or slices. Divide the basil leaves and the strawberries between the plates. Add the tomatoes and the egg halves.

Add the prawns and the salmon on the plates. Garnish with mashed avocado and dill. Season with Tomato & Pepper seasoning. Cut the lemon in half and squeeze the lemon juice on the salmon, the avocado and the prawns.

SALMON

SALMON ASPARAGUS GRAPES AND BROCCOLI

10 oz (280 g) skinless salmon fillet

3 tbsp olive oil

1 tsp dried thyme

½ tsp salt

1 tsp lemon pepper seasoning

10 broccoli florets

6-8 fresh asparagus spears

8-10 cherry or other small tomatoes

10-14 grapes (cut some in half)

1 small carrot

1 tsp crushed red pepper

(or Tomato & Pepper seasoning)

How to prepare:

Cook the broccoli in boiling water for 6-8 minutes. (Frozen florets take less time to cook.) Cut the salmon in half. Heat up a pan to medium heat. Cook the salmon in olive oil for 3 minutes per side. Season with dried thyme, salt and lemon pepper. Cook the asparagus in boiling water for 5 minutes. Peel the carrot and slice it with a julienne peeler. You can also grate the carrot. Cut the tomatoes in half. Drain the asparagus and the broccoli. Cut some of the asparagus in half lengthwise. Divide the asparagus and the broccoli between two plates. Season with red pepper or Tomato & Pepper seasoning. Add grapes and tomato halves on the plates. Add salmon on both plates.

Sprinkle the carrot slices on the dish. (If you want to, drizzle 2 tsp olive oil on the salmon.)

SALMON AVOCADO AND BROCCOLI

10 oz (280 g) sliced cured salmon
(or smoked salmon)
10 broccoli florets
1 avocado
8-12 grapes
6-10 cherry or other small tomatoes

8-12 baby carrots
6-8 asparagus spears from can (tin)
2 tbsp parmesan flakes
1 tsp lemon pepper seasoning
1 tsp dried thyme
1 lemon

How to prepare:

Cook the broccoli florets in boiling water for 6-8 minutes. If you use cooked frozen baby carrots, cook them on medium heat for 5 minutes. (Fresh baby carrots need 14 minutes to cook).

Cut the avocado in half, remove the stone and use a spoon to get the fruit off the skin. Slice the avocado. Divide the slices between two plates.

Cut the grapes into halves. Cuth the asparagus in half. Divide the salmon between two plates. Drain the broccoli and the carrots. Add these on the plates with the asparagus. Add the tomatoes and the grapes. Sprinkle parmesan flakes on the dish for extra delicious flavor.

Cut the lemon in half and drizzle lemon juice on the salmon and the avocado. Season with lemon pepper seasoning and dried thyme.

SALMON ASPARAGUS CHIVES AND CREAM

11 oz (310 g) sliced cured salmon (or smoked)

4-8 small potatoes

8-10 cherry tomatoes

10 asparagus spears (or green beans)

4 tbsp low-fat sour cream (crème fraiche)

1 tsp Ginger Chili & Lime seasoning

(Substitute: ½ tsp ginger powder and ½ tsp chili)

2 tsp garlic paste (or powder)

2 tbsp chopped dill

1-2 tbsp chopped chives

1 lemon

2 tbsp extra virgin olive oil

1 tsp salt

Optional: 2 tsp dried basil

How to prepare:

Brush and cook the small potatoes in boiling water until they are soft. Cut off the hard bottom part of the asparagus. Cook the asparagus in boiling water for 5 minutes. Cut the tomatoes into halves.

Divide the salmon between two plates. Drain the asparagus and the potatoes when they are soft. Cut the potatoes in half. Cut a few asparagus spears in half lengthwise. Add potatoes on both plates. Season lightly with salt, dried basil and olive oil. Add the tomatoes and the asparagus on the plates. Season with Ginger Chili & Lime seasoning. Season the salmon with lemon juice and garlic.

Sprinkle chives on the plates. Add sour cream on each plate and sprinkle dill on the salmon and the sour cream.

SALMON POTATO TOMATO AND DILL

10 oz (280 g) cured or smoked salmon
2-4 potatoes (small or medium size)
(Substitute: 12 broccoli florets)
¼ tsp salt
12-16 cherry or other small tomatoes

½ small red onion
4-8 green olives
1 lemon
2 tbsp baby capers in brine
(Substitute: 2 tbsp chopped parsely)
Fresh dill

How to prepare:

Peel two potatoes if you have diabetes and four if your diet allows more potatoes. Cook the potatoes in boiling water until they are soft. Sprinkle salt in the cooking water.

If you prefer broccoli to potatoes, cook the florets for 7 minutes. Cut the tomatoes in half. Peel the red onion and use half of it. Chop off the hard root part and slice the onion. Cut some of the olives into slices.

Cut half of the lemon into slices and save the other half for seasoning. Drain the potatoes and cut them in half. Divide the potatoes between two plates. Add salmon on both plates. Add the tomatoes, the onion slices, the lemon slices and the olives. Season with lemon juice.

Garnish with dill and baby capers.

SMOKED SALMON PRAWNS AND MUSHROOM

4-6 new or other small potatoes

10 oz (280 g) hot or cold smoked salmon

8 white mushrooms

2-3 tbsp olive oil

8 cooked, peeled prawns

1 tsp Roasted Garlic & Pepper seasoning

1 tsp lemon pepper seasoning

½ tsp salt

8-10 basil leaves

Optional: 4 tbsp blueberries

How to prepare:

If you have frozen prawns, put them in the refrigerator 1 day before you cook this dish.

Brush or peel the potatoes and cook them until they are soft.

Cut the mushrooms in half or into slices. Cut the smoked salmon fillet in half.

Take a pan and heat it up to medium heat. Add the olive oil and the mushrooms. Cook for 2-3 minutes. Stir occasionally. Season with Garlic & Pepper seasoning (or ground black pepper).

Divide the potatoes, the mushrooms and the salmon between two plates. Add the prawns, the basil and the berries. Season with lemon pepper seasoning. If you have lemon at home, add one slice on each plate.

DID YOU KNOW: WHITE MUSHROOMS ARE LOW IN CALORIES AND SUGAR. THEY ARE ALSO HIGH IN PROTEIN AND VITAMIN D, AND THEY'RE A SOURCE OF VITAMIN B12.

PAK CHOI SALMON BROCCOLINI AND CARROT

11 oz (310 g) skinless salmon fillet

3 tbsp olive oil

1 tsp lemon pepper

½ tsp salt

4 lemon slices

1 carrot

6 pak choi (bok choy) leaves

(Substitute: baby spinach leaves)

8 broccolini stems (or 8 broccoli florets)

1 tsp Tomato & Pepper seasoning

4 tbsp sweet chili sauce

Optional: 4 blueberries & raspberries

How to prepare:

Peel the carrot and cut it into ½ inch (10 mm) slices. Cook the carrot for 7-8 minutes. Cook the broccolini for 2 minutes. (If you have broccoli, cook the florets for 8 minutes.) Cut the pak choi leaves lengthwise. Cut the lemon slices in half and divide these between two plates.

Cut the salmon in half. Take a non-stick pan and cook the salmon fillets in olive oil on medium heat for 1 minute on each four sides. During the last 2 minutes, add the pak choi (or baby spinach) leaves in the pan. Season the salmon with salt and lemon pepper.

Divide the salmon fillets and pak choi between the plates. Add the broccoli and the carrot. Season with Tomato & Pepper seasoning. Add blueberries and raspberries on top of the salmon. Season the pak choi and the broccoli with sweet chili sauce.

DID YOU KNOW: BROCCOLINI IS HIGH IN CALCIUM AND MAGNESIUM, WHICH HELP TO REGULATE YOUR BLOOD PRESSURE. IT IS ALSO HIGH IN FIBER.

SALMON BROCCOLI AND ZUCCHINI

11 oz (310 g) smoked salmon fillet

1 zucchini (courgette)

2 potatoes

6 cherry tomatoes

8 broccoli florets

¼ tsp salt

2 tbsp chopped red onion

1 tsp dried basil

1 tsp lemon pepper seasoning

2 tbsp sweet chili sauce

6-8 basil leaves

How to prepare:

Peel the potatoes and cut them into thick slices. Cook these in boiling water until they are soft. Cook the broccoli florets in boiling water for 7 minutes. Season with salt. Cut the hard end off the zucchini (courgette), then cut it into 2-3 pieces crosswise. Now slice the zucchini lengthwise to get 8-10 long slices. Curl the slices and put them in a bowl with cold water.

Divide the potato slices between two plates. Cut the salmon fillet in half and add one piece on each plate. Drain the broccoli. Curl the zucchini slices and add a broccoli floret into each slice. Add these on the plates. Cut the tomatoes into slices. Add the slices on the salmon. Add red onion on the salmon. Season with dried basil (or thyme), lemon pepper and sweet chili. Garnish with basil leaves.

DID YOU KNOW: ZUCCHINI (COURGETTE) IS A FRUIT THAT IS HIGH IN FIBER. HIGH FIBER DIETS HELP IMPROVE HEART HEALTH. ZUCCHINI IS RICH IN THE ANTIOXIDANTS LUTEIN AND ZEAXANTHIN, AS WELL AS VITAMIN K AND MAGNESIUM.

SALMON MUSHROOM TOMATO AND CREAM

10 oz (280 g) skinless salmon fillet
3 tbsp olive oil
½ tsp salt
½ tsp turmeric (or curcumin) powder
1 tsp lemon pepper seasoning
8 mushrooms
1 tsp dried thyme
1 cup (240 g) crispy lettuce

8 cherry tomatoes
4 white asparagus spears from can (tin)
2 tsp balsamic glaze
2 spring onions
1 lemon
½ cup (120 ml) crème fraiche (sour cream)
½ tsp chili paste, ½ tsp ginger paste
Optional: 4 tbsp blueberries

How to prepare:

Cut the salmon into 4 slices. Cook the salmon and the mushrooms in a non-stick pan in oil on medium heat. Cook for 3 minutes, then turn the salmon and cook for 2-3 minutes. Stir occasionally. Season the salmon with salt, turmeric powder and lemon pepper seasoning. Sprinkle dried thyme on the mushrooms.

Slice the lettuce. Divide the lettuce between two plates. Cut the tomatoes in half. Cut the asparagus into smaller pieces. Add the tomatoes and the asparagus on the plates and season with balsamic glaze. Divide the salmon and the mushrooms between the plates. Squeeze the juice of 1 lemon on the salmon. Cut the spring onions into thin slices and sprinkle these on the plates. Mix the crème fraiche with chili and ginger. Add the sauce on the salmon. Decorate with blueberries, if you have some at home.

SALMON FIGS FETA AND PEAR

11 oz (310 g) skinless salmon fillet
3 tbsp olive oil
½ tsp salt
1 tsp lemon pepper seasoning
½ tsp chili powder
¼ cup (60 ml) white wine or water
1 tomato
2 tbsp thyme leaves

½ cup (120 ml) crème fraiche (sour cream)
1 tsp chili paste
2 figs
½ cup (120 g) pear slices
4-8 olives
4 tbsp feta cheese cubes
Balsamic glaze
Optional: redcurrant berries

How to prepare:

Cut the salmon into 1 inch (25 mm) pieces. Take a pan and cook the salmon in oil for 4 minutes on medium heat. Turn the fish once per minute. Add the white wine (or water) when you have cooked for 3 minutes. Season with salt, lemon pepper and chili.

Divide the salmon between two plates. Cut the tomatoes into slices. Add the slices and the thyme leaves on the plates. Mix the chili paste with the crème fraiche (sour cream). Add the sauce on the fish. Cut each fig into 4 wedges and add these on the plates. Cut the pear slices in half and place around the fish. Add feta cheese and olives.

Drizzle balsamic glaze on the figs. If you have redcurrant or other berries at home, add some for extra lovely flavor.

SALMON FETA BACON AND BERRIES

10 oz (280 g) skinless salmon fillet
(Substitute: white lean fish fillet)
3 tbsp olive oil
1 tsp salt
1 tsp lemon pepper seasoning
1 lemon
Optional: 4 slices of bacon

½ cup (120 g) lettuce slices
10 cherry tomatoes
1 tsp dried thyme
1 tsp chili paste (or chili powder)
½ cup (120 g) feta cheese cubes
2 radishes
Optional: 20 blueberries

How to prepare:

Slice the radishes and cut the tomatoes in half. Divide lettuce, tomatoes and radish slices between two plates. Add the feta cheese and dried thyme on the vegetables.

Cut the salmon (or the white fish) fillet into 4 pieces. Take a non-stick pan and cook the fish in olive oil on medium heat for 3 minutes. Turn the fillets, lower the heat to medium low and cook for 3 more minutes. Season with salt and lemon pepper seasoning. Place the salmon on the plates.

Cut the lemon in half and squeeze the juice of half a lemon on the salmon. Season the salmon with chili paste for extra lovely flavor. Cut the other half of the lemon into slices. Pan fry the bacon slices as crispy as you like them. Add two slices of bacon on each dish. Garnish with lemon slices and blueberries!

WHITE LEAN FISH

PIKE PERCH MUSHROOM AND ASPARAGUS

10 oz (280 g) pike perch fillet
4 tbsp olive oil
6 white asparagus spears from can (tin)
6 white mushrooms
1 cup (240 g) chopped lettuce
2 tomatoes and 1 lemon

Optional: 2 tsp baby capers
½ tsp salt and 1 tsp dried thyme
1 tsp lemon pepper seasoning
4 tbsp fresh dill
2-4 tbsp balsamic glaze
Optional: 8-10 basil leaves, 2 tsp pesto

WHITE FISH: pike perch, cod, Alaska pollock, bass or pike!

How to prepare:

Divide the chopped lettuce between two plates. Cut the tomatoes into wedges and add these on the lettuce. Cut 4 slices from the lemon's middle part. Cut the slices in half. Add 4 halves per plate.

Cut the fish fillet into 2-4 pieces. Cut the mushrooms into slices. Take a non-stick pan and cook the fish and the mushroom on medium heat in olive oil for 6 minutes. Turn the fish after 3 minutes. Add 5 tbsp of water if needed. Season with salt, lemon pepper and dried thyme.

Divide the fish and the mushrooms between the plates. Cut the asparagus spears in half. Add asparagus and baby capers on the plates. Squeeze the rest of the lemon juice on the fish and the vegetables. Season with balsamic glaze, dill, basil and pesto.

PIKE PERCH APPLE MUSHROOM AND POTATO

4-6 small potatoes

11 oz (310 g) pike perch fillet (or similar)

½ tsp salt

1 tsp lemon pepper seasoning

4 tbsp olive oil

6 large mushrooms

1 small red onion and 1 lemon

4 peeled garlic cloves

4 tbsp sliced leek

1 apple

2 tsp baby capers

¼ cup (60 ml) white wine or vegetable stock

1 tsp chili paste

Optional: 10 sun-dried tomato slices

Optional: 6 broccolini stems

1-2 tbsp fresh dill

How to prepare:

Heat up the oven to 410 F (210 C). Scrub the potatoes and cut them in half. Cook the potato in boiling water for 5 minutes. Wash the apple and cut it into pieces, removing the inner hard part at the same time. Cut the mushrooms into quarters. Cut the lemon into wedges. Peel the onion and cut it into wedges. Mix white wine (or stock) and chili paste. Add the potatoes, the mushrooms, the sun-dried tomatoes, the onion, the broccolini, the garlic, and the apple in an oven oven pan and cook for 21-24 minutes. Add the white wine (or stock) after the first 12 minutes.

Cut the fish fillet into four pieces. Pan-fry the fish in olive oil on medium heat 3 minutes per side. Season with salt and lemon pepper seasoning. Divide vegetables, apple and potatoes between two plates and add the fish on top. Add the leek, the capers and the dill. Use 2 lemon wedges to squeeze juice on the fish. Add 1 lemon wedge on each plate.

ROLLED FISH CREAM CHEESE AND BERRIES

4-6 small potatoes

10 oz (280 g) white fish fillet

½ tsp salt, ½ tsp chili powder

2 tbsp cream cheese (natural, garlic or herbs)

2 tbsp olive oil

1 tsp Roasted Garlic & Pepper seasoning

¼ cup (60 ml) mild vegetable stock

½ cup (120 ml) low-fat cream

20 cooked, peeled shrimp

Optional: 2 tsp chili paste

1 tsp Tomato & Pepper seasoning

2 tbsp dill

2 tbsp blueberries

2 tbsp sun-dried tomato slices

Optional: 1 tbsp thyme leaves

WHITE FISH: pike perch, cod, Alaska pollock, bass or pike!

How to prepare:

If you use frozen shrimp, put them in the refrigerator 1 day before you cook this dish. Choose any white lean fish fillet. I used pike perch for this dish. Spread low-fat cream cheese on the fish fillets. Season with dill and chili powder. Cut the fillets in half, roll them and use a toothpick to keep each roll closed while cooking. Cook the potatoes until they are soft. Heat up a non-stick pan to medium heat and cook the fish in olive oil. Turn the rolls once every minute. Season with salt and Garlic & Pepper seasoning. After 5 minutes, lower the temperature to medium low, add stock and cream. Let simmer for 2 minutes. Add 5 tbsp water and the shrimp. Let simmer for 2 minutes.

Divide the fish and the sauce between two plates. Remove the toothpicks. Add the potatoes. Season with chili paste and Tomato & Pepper seasoning. Garnish with dill and thyme. Add sun-dried tomato slices and blueberries for extra lovely taste.

WHITE FISH TOMATO CUCUMBER AND ORANGE

11 oz (310 g) skinless white fish fillet
½ tsp salt
1 tsp lemon pepper seasoning
1 tsp dried thyme
3 tbsp olive oil
2-3 tbsp dill

½ cucumber
12 cherry tomatoes
½ leek
½ orange
2 slices of a lemon
10-14 basil leaves

WHITE FISH: pike perch, cod, Alaska pollock, bass or pike!

How to prepare:

Cut the fish fillet into 4 slices. Cook these in a pan on medium heat in olive oil. Cook two minutes per side. Season with salt, dried thyme and lemon pepper seasoning.

Peel the cucumber and cut it into slices. Divide these between two plates.

Cut the orange into wedges. Wash the leek and cut it into thin slices. Divide the tomatoes between the plates. Add fish on both plates and sprinkle leek on the fish and around it.

Divide the tomatoes and the orange wedges between the plates. Add basil leaves on both plates and sprinkle dill on the dish. Cut the lemon slices in half and add two halves on both plates.

If you want more protein, add hummus or cashew nuts (unsalted).

CHICKEN

CHICKEN MOZZARELLA AND TOMATO

6 chicken inner fillets
3 tbsp olive oil
½ tsp curcumin powder (or turmeric)
½ tsp salt
½ tsp chili powder
(or ground black pepper)
1 mozzarella cheese ball

1 cup (240 g) chopped mixed lettuce
2 tbsp chopped chives
Optional: 4-8 small basil leaves
10 cherry tomatoes
2 tsp extra virgin olive oil
1 tsp Roasted Garlic & Pepper seasoning
(Substitute: ground black pepper)

How to prepare:

Take a pan and heat it up to medium heat. Add the olive oil and the chicken fillets. Cook for 3 minutes. Flip the fillets. Season with salt, curcumin and chili. Add 6 tbsp of water. Cook for 3 more minutes.

Divide the chopped lettuce between two plates. Cut the mozzarella into 4 slices. Cut the small tomatoes into slices or in half. Add mozzarella and tomatoes on each plate. Cut the chicken fillets into smaller pieces and divide these between the plates. Season with olive oil and chopped chives. Add basil leaves if you have some at home. Season with Garlic & Pepper seasoning.

TERIYAKI CHICKEN AND NOODLES

3 oz (80 g) whole wheat noodles

½ tsp curcumin

4-6 chicken inner fillets

(Substitute: 8 large mushrooms)

4 tbsp olive oil

½ cup (120 ml) teriyaki sauce

1 tsp chili paste (or chili powder)

1 small carrot

10 broccoli florets

Optional: Chinese broccoli

(also called soy chum and gai lan)

How to prepare:

Cook the noodles according to the instructions on the package. Peel the carrot and chop off the hard ends. Cut the carrot into small pieces. Cook the carrot and the broccoli in the same pot in boiling water until they are soft.

When the noodles are ready, divide them between two plates or bowls (without the cooking water). Cut the chicken fillets lengthwise in half. Cut the slices in half. (If you choose to use mushrooms, cut these into 1 inch (25 mm) pieces.) Cook the chicken (mushrooms) in olive oil on medium heat for 2 minutes. Stir occasionally. Lower the temperature to medium-low. Add the teriyaki sauce and cook for 3 minutes. Stir occasionally. If you like spicy food, add chili to the sauce. If you can find Chinese broccoli, wash the leaves and add these to the sauce. Add also the carrot. Let simmer for 1 minute.

Add the chicken sauce on the noodles. Garnish with broccoli florets.

CHICKEN TOMATO AND ASPARAGUS

6 chicken inner fillets
1 tbsp parsley
1 tbsp thyme leaves
1 tsp minced garlic
1 tbsp olive oil for the marinade
1 tbsp lemon juice
3 tbsp olive oil for the chicken

2 tsp soy sauce
1 cup (240 g) chopped mixed lettuce
2 tbsp pickled red onion (or fresh red onion slices)
4 asparagus spears from can (jar)
8 small tomatoes
2 tbsp vinegar (apple cider or honey)

How to prepare:

Add parsley, thyme leaves, olive oil, garlic and lemon juice in a mortar and crush until you have a nice thick marinade. Drizzle the marinade on the chicken fillets.

Divide the chopped lettuce between two plates. Add the pickled red onion (or fresh onion slices). Cut the asparagus spears into smaller pieces and add them on the lettuce. Cut the tomatoes in half and divide these between the plates. Season with vinegar.

Take a pan and heat it up on medium heat. Add the olive oil and the chicken fillets. Cook for 3 minutes. Turn the fillets, add 6 tbsp water and the soy sauce. Lower the temperature to medium low. Cook for 3 minutes and stir lightly twice. If needed, add a little bit of water into the pan. When the chicken is ready, take the pan off the stove and let the chicken rest for 1 minute. Add the fillets on the plates next to the salad.

CHICKEN ARUGULA TOMATO AND BERRIES

8 chicken inner fillets

4 tbsp olive oil

2 tsp soy sauce

1 tsp garlic paste

½ tsp curcumin powder (or turmeric)

½ tsp ground black pepper

A handful of arugula leaves

A handful of chopped lettuce

10-14 cherry tomatoes

Optional: 6-8 green olives

1 spring onion (scallion)

Optional: ½ cup (120 g) blueberries

How to prepare:

Cut the chicken fillets into 1 inch (25 mm) pieces. Take a pan and heat it up to medium heat. Add the olive oil and the chicken. Cook for 3 minutes. Stir and turn the chicken twice a minute. Season with soy sauce, pepper, curcumin and garlic. Add a little bit of water. Cook for 2 more minutes.

Wash the arugula leaves and divide them and the chopped lettuce between two plates. Cut the tomatoes in half. Add the tomatoes and the olives on the plates.

Divide the chicken between the plates. Wash the spring onion. Chop off the hard bottom part and cut the white part of the onion into slices. Add these and the blueberries on the plates.

CHICKEN ASPARAGUS FETA AND TOMATO

4 chicken inner fillet

3 tbsp olive oil

½ tsp salt

½ tsp curcumin powder

4-6 green asparagus spears

1 cup (240 g) mixed chopped lettuce

10 cherry tomatoes

4 garlic cloves

4 tbsp feta cheese cubes (or salad cheese)

1 tsp Tomato & Pepper seasoning (or similar)

4 tbsp extra virgin olive oil

2 tsp lemon pepper seasoning

Optional: 12-14 basil leaves

How to prepare:

Cut off the hard end of the asparagus, then cut the spears in half and cut the halves lengthwise (if they are thick). Cook these in boiling water for 4-5 minutes.

Cook the chicken fillets in oil on medium heat for 3 minutes. Turn the fillets and cook for 3 more minutes. If the pan gets dry, add a little bit of water. Season with salt and curcumin.

Divide the chopped lettuce between two plates. Wash the tomatoes and cut them into slices. Add these on the lettuce. Peel the garlic cloves and add a few on each plate. Cut the chicken fillets into slices and add on the plates. Divide the asparagus between the plates. Season with Tomato & Pepper seasoning (or your favorite spice).

Divide the cheese between the plates. Season with lemon pepper. Drizzle olive oil on the salads and garnish with basil leaves.

CHICKEN TOMATO PARMESAN SPAGHETTI

4 chicken inner fillets

2 tbsp chopped parsley

1 tsp minced garlic

1 tbsp olive oil for the marinade

1 tbsp lemon juice

3 tbsp olive oil for cooking

3 oz (85 g) whole grain spagehtti

(substitute: fusilli, penne or farfalle)

8-10 cherry or other small tomatoes

4 tbsp extra virgin olive oil

2 tbsp parmesan flakes

2 tsp dried basil or thyme

How to prepare:

Cook the pasta. Follow the instructions on the package.

Put parsley, olive oil and garlic in a mortar and crush until you have a nice thick sauce. Add the lemon juice and stir. Drizzle the marinade on the fillets.

Take a pan and cook the chicken fillets for 3 minutes in oil on medium heat. Lower the temperature to medium low and turn the fillet. Cook for 3 minutes. Add a little bit of water if the pan gets too dry. Stir lightly a few times.

Drain the pasta and divide it between two plates. Cut the chicken fillets into smaller pieces. Add these on the pasta. Cut the tomatoes in half and add tomatoes on the pasta.

Drizzle lightly with olive oil. Sprinkle parmesan flakes and dried herbs on the pasta.

CHICKEN FETA TOMATO AND PASTA

2 chicken inner fillet

3 tbsp olive oil

1 tsp ground black pepper

3 oz (85 g) fusilli or farfalle pasta

½ tsp salt

6 cherry tomatoes

1 cup (240 g) chopped mixed lettuce

4 tbsp feta cheese cubes (or salad cheese)

2 tbsp chopped chives

2 tsp dried basil

2 tsp dried oregano

Optional: ½ cucumber

How to prepare:

Cook the pasta. Follow the instructions on the package.

Take a pan and cook the chicken fillets for 3 minutes in oil on medium heat. Turn the fillet and cook the other side for 3 minutes. Season with salt and black pepper. Add 5 tbsp water if the pan gets too dry. Stir lightly a few times.

Drain the pasta. Divide the chopped lettuce and the pasta between two plates. Cut the chicken into small pieces. Add the chicken and the cheese cubes on the salads. Cut the tomatoes in half and add these on the plates. Season with chopped chives and dried herbs. If you have half a cucumber, peel it, and cut it into slim sticks. Add the sticks in the salads.

(Whole-grain pasta is a better choice for many, as it is lower in calories and carbs but higher in fiber and nutrients. However, in addition to the type of pasta you pick, what you top it with is just as important.)

MEAT

PESTO PORK MUSHROOM AND CASHEW

12 oz (340 g) pork tenderloin

3 tbsp olive oil

½ tsp salt

2 tsp Tomato & Pepper seasoning (or similar)

1 small can (tin) of mushrooms

6 tbsp white wine or water

½ small leek

4 tsp green pesto

12-16 basil leaves

10 cherry tomatoes

10-20 cashew nuts

4 tbsp parmesan cheese flakes

Balsamic glaze

Optional: 10 strawberries

How to prepare:

Heat up the oven to 410 F (210 C). Clean the pork tenderloin and cut it in half. Pan-fry the pork halves in olive oil for 1 minute on each four sides on medium high heat. Transfer the pork to an oven pan. Season with salt and Tomato & Pepper seasoning (or black pepper). Add the mushrooms in the oven pan. Put the pan into the oven for 20 minutes. When 15 minutes have passed sprinkle white wine or water on the dish. While the pork is in the oven, cut the tomatoes in half. Cut the strawberries and the leek into slices. When the pork is ready, take it from the oven and let it rest for 2 minutes. Cut the pork into 1 inch (25 mm) slices and divide between two plates. Season the pork with delicious pesto. Divide leek, tomatoes, cashew, strawberries, parmesan flakes and basil leaves between the plates. Drizzle a little bit of balsamic glaze on the tomatoes and the mushrooms.

BEEF TENDERLOIN TOMATO AND SOUR CREAM

- 2 beef tenderloin steaks (6 oz / 170 g each)
- 3 tbsp olive oil
- 1 tsp ground black pepper
- 1 tsp salt
- 1 tsp Roasted Garlic & Pepper seasoning
- 1 tsp soy sauce
- 8 crispy lettuce leaves
- 12 cherry tomatoes
- 2 tbsp sour cream
- ½ tsp Tomato & Pepper seasoning
- 2 tsp extra virgin olive oil
- 6 basil leaves (or 2 tbsp fresh parsley)

How to prepare:

Pan-fry the steaks in oil on medium heat for 3 minutes. Turn the steaks and cook for 3 more minutes. If the pan gets too dry, add a little bit of water in the pan. Add soy sauce in the pan during the last minute you cook the steaks. Season with black pepper, salt and Garlic & Pepper seasoning.

Wash the lettuce leaves and cut them into slices. Divide these between two plates. Add one steak on each plate. Cut the tomatoes in half and place these around the steak.

Add sour cream (or similar) on the steaks. Season with olive oil and Tomato & Pepper seasoning (or your favorite pepper). Chop the basil leaves (or parsley). Sprinkle the chopped herb on the sour cream.

PROSCIUTTO NECTARINE TOMATO PANCAKE

2 large pancakes or 4 small ones
(ready made or use a pancake mixture)
5 oz (140 g) prosciutto (or similar ham)
1 nectarine
14 cherry tomatoes
4 tbsp hummus

½ tsp lemon pepper seasoning
½ cucumber
2 tsp extra virgin olive oil
1 tsp dried basil
Optional: Balsamic glaze

How to prepare:

The main ingredients for pancakes are plain flour, eggs, milk and a pinch of salt. But each country has their own traditions, so I let you choose which kind of mixture you want to use.

Use ready made pancakes or pan-fry your own pancakes. Divide them between two plates. In this recipe I used two 8 inch (200 mm) pancakes.

Cut the prosciutto into small slices. Wash the tomatoes and cut them in half. Cut the cucumber into slices lengthwise. Add these in cold water. Cut the nectarine into slices.

Spread the hummus on the pancakes. Season with lemon pepper. Divide the prosciutto, the tomatoes and the nectarine slices between the pancakes. Season with dried basil and olive oil. Divide the cucumber slices between the pancakes. Season with lovely balsamic glaze. Glaze is thicker than balsamic vinegar and has a more aromatic flavor. Roll the pancakes and enjoy.

PORK TENDERLOIN MUSHROOM AND TOMATO

11 oz (310 g) pork tenderloin

10 mushrooms cut into halves

4 tbsp olive oil

½ tsp salt

2 tsp Roasted Garlic & Pepper seasoning

2 tsp sweet chili sauce

1 medium size potato

1 tsp Tomato & Pepper seasoning

2 large romaine lettuce leaves

14 cherry tomatoes

½ cup (120 g) peas from can (tin)

½ leek

Optional: 2 tsp pesto

10-14 basil leaves

2 tsp grated parmesan (or similar cheese)

How to prepare:

Peel and cook the potato in boiling water until soft. Clean the pork tenderloin and cut it into 1 inch (25 mm) slices. Pan-fry the pork on medium heat in olive oil for 3 minutes. Turn the fillets, add the mushrooms, and season with salt and the pepper seasoning. Cook for 2 minutes, lower the temperature to medium-low, add a little bit of water, and cook for 2 minutes.

Add one large lettuce leaf on each plate. Cut the tomatoes into slices or halves. Add tomato, basil and pesto on the lettuce leaves. Cut the leek into thin slices and divide these and the peas between the lettuce leaves. When the potato is soft cut it into 4 wedges. Add two wedges on each plate. Season the wedges with Tomato & Pepper seasoning. Spinkle parmesan on the potatoes. Divide the white meat fillets between the plates and add the mushrooms on the meat. Season with sweet chili sauce.

BEEF TENDERLOIN PEAS AND POTATO

2 beef tenderloin steaks (6 oz / 170 g each)

3 tbsp olive oil

½ tsp salt

1 tsp Tomato & Pepper seasoning

1 tsp Garlic & Pepper seasoning

8 tbsp cooking cream for the steaks

1 medium size potato

1 tsp ground black pepper

1 tsp garlic powder

4 tbsp cooking cream for the potato

6 grapes

6 cherry tomatoes

½ cup (120 g) lettuce slices

½ cup (120 g) peas (frozen)

Optional: 20 blueberries

How to prepare:

Cut the potato into ½ inch (10 mm) slices and cook these in boiling water until they are soft. Drain the potatoes and drizzle cream on them and season with garlic and ground black pepper. Put the lid on the pot.

Pan-fry the steaks in olive oil on medium high heat for 1 minute. Lower the temperature to medium heat and cook for 2 minutes. Turn the steaks and cook for 2 more minutes. Lower the temperature to medium low, add cream in the pan and let simmer for 30 seconds. Season with salt and the pepper seasonings.

Warm up the frozen peas in boiling water for 2 minutes. Divide the potatoes and the lettuce between two plates. Add tomatoes and grapes on both plates. Add one steak on each plate. Add a little cream from the pan on the steaks. Add the peas next to the steaks.

DESSERT

BERRY SOUP MANGO CREAM AND BERRIES

1 cup ready made berry soup (or make your own)

4 mango (or peach) slices from can (jar)

2 tbsp blueberries (or strawberries)

2 tbsp whipped cream

How to prepare:

Divide the berry soup between two dessert bowls. If you can't find ready made berry soup in the store, here is an easy to do recipe:

1 cup (240 ml) mixed frozen berries, 3 tbsp sugar and 1 cup (240 ml) water

1 tbsp potato starch or corn flour and 2 tbsp cold water.

Place the frozen berries, water and sugar in a medium size saucepan and bring to a boil without stirring. Whisk the potato flour with the water in a small bowl and add the paste (stirring slowly) into the berry soup. Let the soup come "to bubble", and then take the pan off the heat. Let the soup cool down for 30 minutes.

Cut the mango slices into small pieces. Add most slices on the berry soup.

Add whipped cream on the mango. Add the rest of the mango pieces. Garnish with blueberries.

APPLE NECTARINE PANCAKE AND CREAM

2 pancakes
(ready made or use a pancake mixture)
1 nectarine

2-4 tbsp apple sauce from can (jar)
2-4 tbsp whipped cream
2 tbsp frozen blueberries

How to prepare:

Place the frozen blueberries in a small bowl with cold water.

The main ingredients for pancakes are plain flour, eggs, milk and a pinch of salt. But each country has their own traditions, so I let you choose which kind of mixture you want to use.

Use ready made pancakes or pan-fry your own pancakes. Divide them between two plates. I made this time two 6 inch (150 mm) pancakes.

Add apple sauce on the pancakes. Cut the nectarine into slices. Cut two of the slices into small pieces. Divide the nectarine between the pancakes. Add whipped cream on both pancakes. Drain the blueberries and add these on the cream.

STRAWBERRY NECTARINE AND CREAM

10 strawberries

1 nectarine

10 tbsp whipped cream

Optional: 1/4 tsp vanilla sugar

How to prepare:

Make whipped cream or use ready made. Add vanilla sugar to the cream, if you want to enjoy an extra lovely flavor. Divide the whipped cream between two dessert plates or bowls.

Cut the green part off the strawberries. Cut the berries into halves.

Cut the nectarine into slices.

Divide the strawberries and the nectarine slices between the plates.

This is a very easy to do dessert, which you can do any day of the week. If you want to add more ingredients to this dessert, try thin banana slices or blueberries.

MANDARIN BERRIES PEACH AND CREAM

8 peach slices from can (jar)
10 raspberries
10-14 blueberries

1 mandarin
8 tbsp whipped cream
(Substitute: vanilla cream or yogurt)

How to prepare:

Peel the mandarin and cut the slices in half. Cut the peach slices in half. Divide half of the mandarin and peach slices between two dessert bowls. Add 2 tbsp whipped cream in each bowl.

Add half of the berries in each bowl and divide the rest of the whipped cream between the dessert bowls.

Add the rest of the fruit slices and the berries on top of the whipped cream.

HEALTHY FOOD

Protein is an incredibly important part of our diet and nutrition. Chickpeas, tofu, almonds and hummus are great sources of protein, if you don't eat meat, chicken or fish.

Heart-healthy food: Beans, chickpeas, lentils, nuts, fish, seafood, eggs and poultry are protein-rich foods that can be enjoyed as part of a heart-healthy diet. Tomato, avocado, almond, kiwi, onion, low-fat cheese and dairy products, berries, olive oil, herbs, wholegrain products and lean meat are heart-healthy food.

Foods to boost your eye health: Eggs, citrus fruit, beans, carrot, nuts, fish, sweet potatoes, salmon and green vegetables are healthy food, which also boost your eye health. Especially orange-colored vegetables and fruits have vitamin A, which is very important for the retina and helps moisten the eyes. Vitamin C is just as important. For example broccoli, bell peppers, tomatoes and fruit contain vitamin C. Avocado, salmon and almonds are rich in vitamin E. You can't do anything about your age or family history, but you can change your diet. Some research shows that eating foods high in antioxidants like vitamins A, C and E may help prevent cataracts.

Add these to your diet: tomatoes, carrot, sweet potatoes, cantaloupe melon, apricots, oranges, lemon, peaches, almonds, strawberries, avocados, almonds and omega-3 fatty acids (salmon, tuna, halibut and trout). Consume also spinach, romaine lettuce, broccoli, peas, kale, lean meat and poultry, as these help to maintain good eye and heart health.

What is mostly needed is to cut down on the intake of sugar and unhealthy fat. Keep added sugars to a minimum. Choose healthy sources of sugar such as fruit and low-fat dairy products. Avoid saturated fat (butter, ghee and coconut oil), and choose unsaturated fats (olive or rapeseed oil, nuts, seeds, or fish.

IF YOU HAVE DIABETES

With diabetes, your body doesn't make enough insulin or can't use it as well as it should. When there isn't enough insulin or cells stop responding to insulin, too much blood sugar stays in your bloodstream.

Diabetes-friendly food: Fruits, vegetables, whole grains, beans, peas, low-fat milk, eggs and cheese. Lean meat, fish, tofu, nuts, berries (especially strawberry and blueberry), leafy greens, tomatoes and onion are also diabetes-friendly food. People with diabetes can safely consume avocados, small portions of potatoes and whole grain pasta as part of a healthy eating plan. When you are uncertain of your daily diet needs, it is always wise to consult your doctor.

The secret is to eat small portions of potatoes, whole grain pasta and bread, and focus on a healthy topping. Many skip potatoes, though it is not necessary. Potatoes contain vitamins and potassium. The American Diabetes Association (ADA) recommend eating starchy vegetables, such as potatoes, as part of a healthful diet. Starch is a complex carbohydrate that takes the body longer to break down than simple sugars.

Salmon is perhaps the highest-recommended fish for diabetics, as it's one of the most abundant sources of omega-3 fatty acids. Also halibut contains omega-3 fatty acids.

Another healthy fish is white lean fish. White fish are low in fat, making them one of the healthier, low-fat alternatives to red or processed meat. Enjoy pike perch, cod, Alaska pollock, bass or pike at least once a week.

Milton Keynes UK
Ingram Content Group UK Ltd.
UKHW050924191124
451074UK00029B/150